Roller Bottles for Essential Oils

200++ Roller Bottle Recipes for a Healthy Mind, Body and Soul

Rica V. Gadi

http://oilnaturalempress.com/

DISCLAIMER: This document is a compilation of recipes used successfully by EO enthusiasts who use only high-quality, therapeutic-grade essential oils as determined by many factors including growth, growth location, harvesting process, distillation method used, etc. Please be advised that not all essential oils are created equally, and not all essential oils are suitable for topical use or ingestion. Please do your research before choosing the brand(s) of essential oils you decide to use as well as supplies you use. Always follow label directions on the essential oil bottles.

All the recipes in this book have been inspired by essential oil believers. However, we are not medical practitioners and cannot diagnose, treat or prescribe treatment for any health condition or disease. Just a precaution, before using any alternative medicines, natural supplements, or vitamins, you should always discuss the products you are using or intend to use with your doctor, especially if you are pregnant, trying to get pregnant or nursing.

All information contained within this book is for reference purposes only, and is not intended to substitute advice given by a pharmacist, physician or other licensed health-care professional. As such, the author is not responsible for any loss, claim or damage arising from use of the essential oil recipes contained herein.

This book is dedicated to all the strong people who are taking responsibility of your own well being and doing something to be better.

All my heartfelt gratitude to the following people: my mom Ruby Jane, you have made me everything I am today; my dad Nestor-- my eternal, my angel, and the source of my perseverance; Mommyling, my spiritual guide ; Ria & Joe, the true witnesses of my transformation and my foundation pillars; Ellie Jane, the sparkle of our eyes;

Juan, thanks for always encouraging me to push harder - you are my ONE; Rocco & Radha, my reason for everything.

The Love of my family and friends is the fountain of inspiration that never runs dry. Thank you for constantly inspiring me, motivating me, and loving me unconditionally.

This book will never be complete without the help of my trusted and talented friends: Golda, Jessica, Lika and BFFs at NOW for the moral support.

Blending Essential Oils in a Roller Bottle is the most convenient method to enjoy EOs with very little risk of an allergic reaction.

When the "Oil Recipe Bible" came out, people started to ask me about recipes only for roller bottles.

This is why I decided to put together this Roller Bottles for Essential Oils recipe book. All the recipes in this book are all for blending EOs in a roller bottle..

Remember this is a roller bottle recipe book and should not be used for any blends like diffusers, inhalers, sprays and scrubs as those will use a different dilution than the ones for roller bottles.

Enjoy, and I am sure in a matter of time, your oil blending habit will be a more permanent part of your days, if it isn't already. Happy Blending :)

Table of Contents

Blending Essential Oils in a Roller Bottle
Some Tidbits You Need To Know

Essential Oils are usually super concentrated and too hard to measure how much to actually put straight from the bottle.

Roller bottles are a way that you are able to create blends ready to use with the right dilution. It allows your EO to last longer.

It also makes it easier to apply exactly where you want to target without getting it all over the place.

It is handy and easy to carry in your purse, ready to use at any time you want to.

I like to apply EOs at the bottom of the feet for many reasons. Our feet have bigger pores than any other skin in our bodies. this means that they are able to suck in the therapeutic compounds in our blend into the bloodstream faster that any other parts of the body. Imagine comparing a normal straw to an oversized straw and how much more you can suck in with the latter. This is how the soles of our feet is compared to the rest of the skin in our bodies.

The skin on our feet is also less sensitive and is designed to withstand some abuse. The risk of having an irritation from EOS is less likely to happen when applied on the feet.

The feet don't have the glands that act as a barrier. Sebaceous glands are glands in our skin that produces an oily substance called Sebum, for the purpose of lubricating and waterproofing the skin. Since this is oil and if you put oil on top of oil, it can act as a barrier or it may slow down penetration.

The feet and palms of our hands are the only skin that don't have these, so it is ideal to apply Essential Oils to the feet for maximum penetration.

Now, it would be hard to apply oils directly and very mess, right? Roller bottles make it super easy and convenient to roll the EOs at the bottom of our feet.

Carrier Oils Info

Carrier oils are vegetable-based oils with their own healing properties that dilute essential oils used to help carry the EOs into the skin.

Essential oils are highly concentrated and could evaporate very quickly. The carrier oil is mixed with the essential oil so it could penetrate the skin before it actually evaporates. Although EOs are oils, it is actually not that oily. When mixed with a carrier oil, it allows you to have more of the essential oil into your skin without wasting EOS to evaporate, making the healing properties of the EO strong and more effective.

There are also Essential oils that are too strong to apply directly to the skin and may cause damage, so it is important to dilute them with a carrier oil.

Never add Carrier Oils to your diffuser. This may cause your diffuser to malfunction. Clean your diffuser at least 3 times a week with warm water and natural soap to ensure the diffuser is well maintained and bacteria and mold does not accumulate.

Carrier Oils

There are a lot of different carrier oils that you can use with EOs to dilute them in a roller bottle.

To name a few :

Almond Oil - moisturizing and stays liquid at room temperature. Do not use if you are allergic to nuts.

Apricot Kernel Oil - moisturizing and suitable for sensitive skin or kids. It is super gentle on the skin.

Avocado Oil - moisturizing and suitable for sensitive and damaged skin. Perfect for skin problems.Can be mixed with other carrier oils

Castor Oil - with antibacterial, antiviral and antifungal properties, use topically to eliminate pain and relieve skin irritation.

Coconut Oil - its antibacterial, antiviral and antifungal properties it is the best and most versatile for skin care. The skin absorbs this very quickly. It solidifies in room temp and may still have a slight coconut oil aroma in it - but you can get a fractionated coconut oil to eliminate the 2 challenges above.

Grapeseed Oil - not just for cooking but also great for topical application on the skin.

Jojoba Oil - one of my faves for skin care blends. This oil is the closest to our natural oil our skin produces to it is absorbed easily without being oily. Also amazing for massage oil blends.

Olive Oil - this is the oil for herb type oils. mostly used for cooking but can also be applied to the skin but would need to be blended with a carrier oil that is mild and absorb well with the skin.

Rosehip Seed Oil - super good for deep moisturizing or skin irritations. This oil has a high content of antioxidants and helps remedy dry, scarred and wounded skin.

Recommended Roller Bottle Dilution Guide

RECOMMENDED ROLL-ON BOTTLE DILUTION AMOUNTS

5 ml (1/6 oz.) Roll-on Bottle = ~100 drops (1tsp.)
10 ml (1/3 oz.) Roll-on Bottle = ~200 drops (2 tsp.)
30 ml. (1 oz.) Roll-on Bottle = ~600 drops (6 tsp.)

Roll-on Size	5 ml	10 ml	30 ml	Add EO drops to roll-on, then fill with carrier oil.	
Essential Oil Drops	1	2	6	1%	Dilution Percentage
	2	4	12	2%	
	3	6	18	3%	
	5	10	30	5%	
	10	20	60	10%	
	20	40	120	20%	
	25	50	150	25%	
	50	100	300	50%	

General Guidelines:
Birth to 12 months = .3-.5% dilution
1-5 years = 1.5-3% dilution
6-11 years = 1.5-5% dilution
12-17 years = 1.5-20% dilution
18 years and older = 1.5% dilution-Neat (no dilution)
Elderly or Sensitive Skin = 1-3% dilution
Daily Use = 2-5% dilution
Short Term Use = 10-25% dilution
Local Skin or Systemic Issues = 50% dilution-Neat

These are general guidelines suggestions--not absolute rules--based on traditional aromatheraphy practice.
(Kurt Schnaubelt PhD, Valerie Worwood, Robert Tisserand)

Dilution Basics:

How much you dilute your EO depends on different factors such as weight, sensitivity, health conditions, EOs that are blended in or how long that blend has been used for. There is never an absolute dilution rule, it is you who knows about your level and tolerance. I feel that it is best to start with a higher dilution percentage and increase EO drops over time.

To make sure your EO is safe, make sure that the oils you use are therapeutic grade and do your research on the source and extraction methods used to produce the oils.

Blending Basics

The First Step : Before you can get into blending oils, you first have to know what the single oils are and what they do. This way when you decide what the purpose of your blend is supposed to be, you'll know which oils you are to use.

When you have decided to choose the purpose of your blend and the oils you can use that will help you achieve this purpose, you can begin layering your oils to complete the blend.

In blending , there are typically 3 layers, Top note, middle note and base note.

Top Notes are oils that evaporate faster and the most noticeable scents. This is the first thing you smell in the blend. They diffuse fast into the air and usually are light, clean and penetrates into the nose. I love citrusy oils for this

Middle Notes are oils are considered the core of the blend. They are the main ingredients and they evenly balance the harmony of the blend.

Base Notes are oils that are in the background. It is the tail end of the aroma, the last ones you smell. They give the blend depth if properly layered and it lingers pleasantly over time. These oils are usually on the heavy side - like in an chorale, the bass voice is deep and robust.

To get started, I think 3-4 oils is good and as you gain experience and feel more comfortable with it you can start adding. So example if you want to make a calming blend, you first choose your Middle Notes, the main ingredient that will give you the results you want. So maybe Roman Chamomile and lavender - both great for calming and relaxation, then you choose a base note - something more robust like cedar wood and then the top note, the light, crisp smell you want to smell first — like lemon.

This will give you a well-rounded, balanced blend that serves its purpose and pleasing to smell.

When making roller bottles, I like to use a 10% dilution for a 10mL roller bottle - which is a total of 20 drops of EO. For starters we can do 10 drops total so you don't waste too much of your oils.

Now that you know which oils to use as your notes you need to know which of these 4 classifications they fall under so you know the amount of oil to use and in what order we blend it in.

When blending oils, it is also important to know at which order you add them to to the blend. This affects how they work together as well as how they chemically combine.

1st Layer - The Personifier
These are middle note oils that serve the purpose of your blend that have very strong and sharp aromas that last the longest. This is about 1%-5% of the blend. So for a 20-drop blend , you only need to use 1 drop of your personifier layer.

2nd Layer - The Enhancer
These, too, are middle notes and just like the first layer serve the purpose of the blend. They have a sharp aroma but not as sharp as the personifier. This is what we call the star of the show. The aroma doesn't last as long as the purifier. These oils make up about 50% - 80% of the blend and the dominant ingredient of the blend. So for a 20-drop blend , you would use 10-16 drops of your enhancer layer.

3rd Layer - The Equalizer
This layer is what creates the balance between all the oils blended. Fragrance is not as sharp as the personifier and the aroma lasts shorter than the first layer. This is about 10%-15% of the blend. So for a 20-drop blend , you would use 2-3 drops of your equalizer layer.

4th Layer - The Modifier
This layer is what gives the blend harmony. It seals the blend into one nice package.These oils are mild and the aroma is short-lived but enough to make the blend whole. This is about 4%-8% of the blend. So for a 20-drop blend , you would use 1-2 drops of your equalizer layer.

Note: you don't have to be religious about the quantities above, these are just guides you can use as benchmarks.

Aroma Type Grouping:

I like to group my EOs by type and here is how I normally group them by:

Floral – Jasmine, Ylang Ylang, Lavender,Neroli, Vanilla, Rose, Geranium

Citrusy – Lemon, Bergamot, Orange, Grapefruit, Lemongrass, Tangerine

Woodsy – Frankincense, Cedarwood, Fir, Sandalwood, Juniper, Cypress,Myrrh

Earth – Patchouli, Angelica, Vetiver, Valerian

Herbs – Black Pepper, Rosemary, Thyme, Tea Tree, Basil, Clary Sage, Marjoram, Oregano

Spices – Cinnamon, Nutmeg, Clove, Cumin, Anise, Cardamom, Ginger

Oils belonging to the same classification usually bend well together. Florals mix well with Woodsy, Citrusy or Spices. I like the blends Citrusy make with spicy and herbs. Woodsy is great with most aromas - it's usually the balancer/equalizer oils. The key is to just keep experimenting to discover your own preferences.

Roller Bottle Blending Order

I normally just start with dropping the drops of oils into the **10mL roller bottle**, then adding the carrier oil up until the shoulder of the bottle. Capping the bottle off with the roller and the bottle cap. Instead of shaking the bottle, i like to roll the bottle between my palms first for a minute or 2 for blending, then finishing it off with a few shakes.

NOTE: All recipes in this book is for a 10mL Roller Bottle. If you have a bigger roller bottle, adjust the number of EO drops based on the size of your bottle.

Roller Bottle Recipes

Allergy Relief

Allergy Combative

Prevent allergies from coming back with this essential oils blend.

4 drops Lavender
4 drops Lemon
4 drops Peppermint

Blend Essential Oils and Fill the rest with your favorite Carrier Oil in a roller bottle. Apply it in the palms of our hands. Cup your hands and deeply inhale. You can also apply to bottoms of feet up or back of neck when needed.

Anti Allergy and Immunity Boost

This helps clear breathing and provides everyone with a healthy immune system.

4 drops Lavender
4 drops Lemon
4 drops Purify
3 drops Frankincense

Blend Essential Oils and Fill the rest with your favorite Carrier Oil in a roller bottle. Apply on throat, behind ears, and bottom of feet.

Breathe Right Immunity
This helps clear breathing and promotes healthy immune system.

3 drops Oregano
5 drops Lemon
4 drops Protective Blend

Blend Essential Oils and Fill the rest with your favorite Carrier Oil in a roller bottle. Apply on throat, behind ears, and bottom of feet.

Swim Ears Helper
This will help deflate the swelling on your ear.

5 drops Basil
3 drops Lavender
2 drops Lemongrass
2 drops Peppermint

Blend Essential Oils and Fill the rest with your favorite Carrier Oil in a roller bottle. Apply it in the palms of our hands. Cup your hands and deeply inhale.

Flu Season Never Came

When you feel signs of aches or a sore throat coming this helps clear breathing and promotes healthy immune system.

4 drops Oregano
8 drops Lemon
6 drops Protective Blend

Blend Essential Oils and Fill the rest with your favorite Carrier Oil in a roller bottle. Apply on throat, behind ears, and bottom of feet.

Anxiety

Say No More To Anx
Calm you mind and body from a tough day from school and work with this essential oil blend.

2 drops Frankincense
2 drops Marjoram
3 drops Geranium
3 drops Clary sage
2 drops Orange

Blend Essential Oils and Fill the rest with your favorite Carrier Oil in a roller bottle. Apply it through a circular motion to the temples and back of neck.

My Energizer Day Pill
Get energized for a productive day at work or school

3 drops Wild Orange
3 drops Frankincense
3 drops Cinnamon

Blend Essential Oils and Fill the rest with your favorite Carrier Oil in a roller bottle. Apply on wrists or back of neck as desired

Strong Woman Roar

Lack of courage? This essential oils blend is perfect for you.

3 drops Inner Child
3 drops Grounding
3 drops Present Time
4 drops Valor or Valor II

Blend Essential Oils and Fill the rest with your favorite Carrier Oil in a roller bottle. Apply on wrists or back of neck as desired

Heartbreak Fixer

This will help you ease the pain of a broken heart.

3 drops Harmony
3 drops Forgiveness
3 drops Release
3 drops Lavender

Blend Essential Oils and Fill the rest with your favorite Carrier Oil in a roller bottle. Apply on wrists or back of neck as desired

Jumping for Joy

Uplift your spirit with this essential oils blend.

4 drops Clary Sage
2 drops Fennel
4 drops Lavender
2 drops Geranium
2 drops Peppermint

Blend Essential Oils and Fill the rest with your favorite Carrier Oil in a roller bottle. Apply on wrists or back of neck as desired

Aroma

Awesome Mornings
Get equipped first thing in the morning for you to have an awesome day ahead.

1 drops Joy
3 drops Peppermint
4 drops Lemon
4 drops Orange

Blend Essential Oils and Fill the rest with your favorite Carrier Oil in a roller bottle. Apply it on the wrists.

Digest Ease
Helps you take away the feeling of digestive discomfort.

8 drops DiGize
5 drops Peppermint

Blend Essential Oils and Fill the rest with your favorite Carrier Oil in a roller bottle. Apply it on the wrists.

Yoga Blessing
This blend is perfect for prayer time & yoga.

3 drops Sandalwood
3 drops Ylang Ylang
3 drops Patchouli
3 drops Frankincense
1 drops Vetiver

Blend Essential Oils and Fill the rest with your favorite Carrier Oil in a roller bottle. Apply it on the wrists.

Sexy Time Baby
This can be a perfume substitute because it helps enhance feelings of love and intimacy.

10 drops Whisper
5 drops Passion

Blend Essential Oils and Fill the rest with your favorite Carrier Oil in a roller bottle. Apply it on the wrists.

Fragrant Girl Relax
This can be fragrance substitute and at the same time provide the relaxing nature needed by our females.

8 drops Clary Sage
6 drops Lavender
2 drops Frankincense

Blend Essential Oils and Fill the rest with your favorite Carrier Oil in a roller bottle. Apply it on the wrists.

Fragrant Girl Relax 2.0 .

6 drops Dragon Time
3 drops Clary Sage
3 drops Orange
3 drops Peppermint

Blend Essential Oils and Fill the rest with your favorite Carrier Oil in a roller bottle. Apply it on the wrists.

Joyful Peace
This essential oils blend helps calm and uplift one's mood at the same time.

5 drops Wild Orange
5 drops Frankincense
3 drops Cedar Wood
3 drops Lavender

Blend Essential Oils and Fill the rest with your favorite Carrier Oil in a roller bottle. Apply it on the wrists.

Enlightenment Sanctuary

This helps support the immune system, clears out overwhelming feelings and hopelessness. It also perfect for spiritual enlightenment as well as releasing anxious thoughts and feelings.

10 drops Frankincense
5 drops Melissa
5 drops Patchouli

Blend Essential Oils and Fill the rest with your favorite Carrier Oil in a roller bottle. Apply it on the wrists.

Beauty

Young and Beautiful
Have that youthful glow back with this essential oils blend.

5 drops Lavender
4 drops Frankincense
4 drop Myrrh

Blend Essential Oils and Fill the rest with your favorite Carrier Oil in a roller bottle. Apply on areas that are affected.

WAHM Glow
Helps mommy get a good night rest and have that youthful glow back once more.

5 drops Lavender
5 drops Lemon
5 drops Frankincense
1 tsp alcohol free unscented witch hazel

Blend Essential Oils and Fill the rest with your Witch Hazel in a roller bottle. Apply on areas that are affected.

Pimple Power Defense
Helps treat mild acne.

5 drops Melaleuca
5 drops Lavender
3 drops Lemongrass

Blend Essential Oils and Fill the rest with your favorite Carrier Oil in a roller bottle. Apply on areas that are affected.

Ageless Nourish
Helps your skin nourished and prevents your skin on aging.

3 drops Frankincense
3 drops Lavender
2 drops Sandalwood
2 drops Helichrysum
2 drops Myrrh

Blend Essential Oils and Fill the rest with your favorite Carrier Oil in a roller bottle. Apply on areas that are affected.

Acne Zapper
Perfect for acne breakouts.

4 drops Palmarosa
4 drops Tea Tree
3 drops Frankincense
3 drops Lavender

Blend Essential Oils and Fill the rest with your favorite Carrier Oil in a roller bottle. Apply on areas that are affected.

Flawlessly Clear Skin

Reduce the dark spots and have that flawless skin with no worries.

5 drops Lavender
5 drops Cypress
5 drops Frankincense

Blend Essential Oils and Fill the rest with your favorite Carrier Oil in a roller bottle. Apply on areas that are affected.

Beard Blessing

This essential oils blend is perfect for every types of beard.

3 drops Patchouli
3 drops Sandalwood
3 drops Clary Sage
3 drops Frankincense
3 drops Cypress

Blend Essential Oils and Fill the rest with your favorite Carrier Oil in a roller bottle. Apply on areas that are affected.

Invisible Varicose and Spider Veins
This helps in blood circulation and strengthening of capillary wall of the blood vessels.

6 drops Cypress
2 drops Helichrysum
2 drops Geranium
2 drops Frankincense

Blend Essential Oils and Fill the rest with your favorite Carrier Oil in a roller bottle. Apply on areas that are affected.

Glowing and Young
This helps on calming and soothing your skin, helps you promote a glowing and youthful complexion.

3 drops Helichrysum
3 drops Frankincense
3 drops Sandalwood
1 drops Rosemary

Blend Essential Oils and Fill the rest with your favorite Carrier Oil in a roller bottle. Apply on areas that are affected.

Forever Young Cellulite Eraser

This will help reduce the appearance of cellulite by decreasing water retention improve blood circulation and eliminate build up of toxins.

4 drops Juniper berry
3 drops Cypress
3 drops Geranium

Blend Essential Oils and Fill the rest with your favorite Carrier Oil in a roller bottle. Apply on areas that are affected.

Youthful Blemish Replenish

This will help the blemishes fade and make you look flawless and replenished.

5 drops Lavender
5 drops Melaleuca or Tea Tree
3 drops Rosemary
2 drops Lemon

Blend Essential Oils and Fill the rest with your favorite Carrier Oil in a roller bottle. Apply on areas that are affected.

Teenage Skin

This will help you even your skin tone and reduce sunspots and the appearance of wrinkles.

3 drops Frankincense
3 drops Helichrysum
4 drops Lavender

Blend Essential Oils and Fill the rest with your favorite Carrier Oil in a roller bottle. Apply on areas that are affected.

Cough & Colds

Family Cough & Cold Remedy
Guard your family from the harsh cough and colds

5 drops OnGuard
5 drops Oregano
5 drops Lemon

Blend Essential Oils and Fill the rest with your favorite Carrier Oil in a roller bottle. Apply on feet when symptoms appear.

Stuffy Nose Clearing
Perfect for clearing nose bridges to prevent it from turning into flu.

10 drops Respiratory Blend
5 drops Lime

Blend Essential Oils and Fill the rest with your favorite Carrier Oil in a roller bottle. Apply over sinuses, above eyebrows, and under the nose.

Stuffed Up Fighter - Double Dose
Perfect for clearing nose bridges to prevent it from turning into flu.

8 drops Respiratory Blend
5 drops Lime

Blend Essential Oils and Fill the rest with your favorite Carrier Oil in a roller bottle. Apply over sinuses, above eyebrows, and under the nose.

Cough Protect
Perfect for cough prevention

5 drops Eucalyptus
3 drops Frankincense
2 drops Lemon

Blend Essential Oils and Fill the rest with your favorite Carrier Oil in a roller bottle. Apply onto chest and/or back. Can also apply to the tops of feet at the bridge of the toes.

Stuffy Nose Bandit
Stuffy and runny nose no more for the whole fam with this awesome essential oils blend.

8 drops Breathe
5 drops Lime

Blend Essential Oils and Fill the rest with your favorite Carrier Oil in a roller bottle. Apply over sinus, temples, and ears when needed.

Clear Lungs

This creates a soothing aroma that can help your respiratory system function well.

7 drops Respiratory Blend
3 drops Eucalyptus
3 drops Frankincense

Blend Essential Oils and Fill the rest with your favorite Carrier Oil in a roller bottle. Apply onto chest and/or back. Can also apply to the tops of feet at the bridge of the toes.

Fever Bye Bye

This helps you cool down your temperature when having colds or fever.

5 drops Lemon
5 drops Peppermint
3 drops Frankincense

Blend Essential Oils and Fill the rest with your favorite Carrier Oil in a roller bottle. Apply onto chest and/or back. Can also apply to the tops of feet at the bridge of the toes.

Chest Softener

This is great for people who experience constant chest congestion and coughing.

5 drops RC
3 drops Lemon
3 drops Purification
2 drops Thyme

Blend Essential Oils and Fill the rest with your favorite Carrier Oil in a roller bottle. Apply onto chest and/or back. Can also apply to the tops of feet at the bridge of the toes.

Emotional Stability

Positive and Grounded
Be grounded and be one with the earth in a positive manner

1 drops Patchouli
1 drops Vetiver
1 drops Lime
5 drops Balance
5 drops Lavender

Blend Essential Oils and Fill the rest with your favorite Carrier Oil in a roller bottle. Apply on wrists or back of neck as desired

Confidently Beautiful
Boost up your self-confidence with this essential oils blend.

6 drops Idaho Blue Spruce
6 drops Hong Kuai

Blend Essential Oils and Fill the rest with your favorite Carrier Oil in a roller bottle. Apply it on the wrists.

Easy Peasy Focus

Help calm your kid's mind and body, increase focus and concentration, and help decrease mental clutters with this essential oil blend.

4 drops Balance
2 drops Patchouli
4 drops Serenity
6 drops Lavender
1 drops Vetiver

Blend Essential Oils and Fill the rest with your favorite Carrier Oil in a roller bottle. Apply it on the wrists.

Elated State

Lift up your mood and enhance the feeling of happiness with this essential oils blend.

4 drops Joy
3 drops Frankincense
3 drops Orange

Blend Essential Oils and Fill the rest with your favorite Carrier Oil in a roller bottle. Apply it on the wrists.

Chill and be Cool

Perfect thing to calm you down after a stressful day

4 drops Lavender
3 drops Clary sage
2 drops Ylang Ylang
1 drops Marjoram

Blend Essential Oils and Fill the rest with your favorite Carrier Oil in a roller bottle. Apply it on the wrists.

Super Kids

This helps boost your child's self-confidence.

3 drops Valor
2 drops Frankincense
2 drops Lavender
2 drops Cedarwood

Blend Essential Oils and Fill the rest with your favorite Carrier Oil in a roller bottle. Apply it on the wrists.

Sugar Rush Tamer
This helps calm your hyperactive children.

3 drops White Angelica
3 drops Bergamot
3 drops Valor
3 drops Orange
2 drops Citrus Fresh

Blend Essential Oils and Fill the rest with your favorite Carrier Oil in a roller bottle. Apply it on the wrists.

Life Cheerleader
This helps you boost up your motivation to get things done/

10 drops Lemon
4 drops Eucalyptus Radiata
3 drops Peppermint
1 drop Cinnamon

Blend Essential Oils and Fill the rest with your favorite Carrier Oil in a roller bottle. Apply it on the wrists.

Anger Release

This is perfect for those who want to release feelings of anger and frustrations.

2 drops Patchouli
2 drops Elevation
2 drops Cedarwood
2 drops Balance
2 drops Basil
2 drops Vetiver

Blend Essential Oils and Fill the rest with your favorite Carrier Oil in a roller bottle. Apply it on the wrists.

I feel SUPER

This will help boost your confidence, energy, creativity, and motivation

3 drops Black Pepper
3 drops Lime
3 drops Wild Orange
3 drops Frankincense

Blend Essential Oils and Fill the rest with your favorite Carrier Oil in a roller bottle. Apply it on the wrists.

Blessed and Grateful
This will help you appreciate the good things in life.

4 drops Bergamot
3 drops Wild Orange
2 drops Geranium
2 drops White Fir

Blend Essential Oils and Fill the rest with your favorite Carrier Oil in a roller bottle. Apply it on the wrists.

Power Up, GO!
Be energized and get going with this essential oil blend.

7 drops Eucalyptus
5 drops Rosemary
3 drops Grapefruit

Blend Essential Oils and Fill the rest with your favorite Carrier Oil in a roller bottle. Apply on your wrist and at the back of your neck.

Gliding Harmoniously

This essential oils blend promotes harmony and balance

3 drops Spruce
3 drops Cedarwood
2 drops Juniper Berry
2 drops White Fir

Blend Essential Oils and Fill the rest with your favorite Carrier Oil in a roller bottle. Apply on your wrist and at the back of your neck.

Focus

Memory Sharpener
Boost your memory retention and concentration with this essential oils blend.

4 drops Lavender
3 drops Lemon
2 drops Rosemary
1 drop Cinnamon

Blend Essential Oils and Fill the rest with your favorite Carrier Oil in a roller bottle. Apply it through a circular motion to the temples, wrists and back of neck.

Laser Sharp Focus
Great remedy for giving you focus on your tasks and everyday life routine.

3 drops Peace and Calming
3 drops Valor
3 drops Vetiver
3 drops Lavender
3 drops Cedarwood

Blend Essential Oils and Fill the rest with your favorite Carrier Oil in a roller bottle. Apply to back of neck, on bones directly behind the ears, or in palms and inhale.

Teachers Be Focused

Help yourself focus on the lesson plans and your students' growth in school with this essential oils blend.

1 1/2 teaspoons fractionated coconut oil
5 drops Lavender
5 drops Basil
5 drops Cypress

Blend Essential Oils and Fill the rest with your favorite Carrier Oil in a roller bottle. Apply to back of neck, on bones directly behind the ears, or in palms and inhale.

My Mind Is Made Up

Losing focus on your daily tasks? This is the perfect solution to your problem.

5 drops Cedarwood
5 drops Lavender
5 drops Vetiver

Blend Essential Oils and Fill the rest with your favorite Carrier Oil in a roller bottle. Apply to back of neck, on bones directly behind the ears, or in palms and inhale.

Mind Declutter

Perfect for gearing up your brain for another set of thinking outside the box day at school or at work

4 drops Rosemary
6 drops Lemon
2 drops Cypress

Blend Essential Oils and Fill the rest with your favorite Carrier Oil in a roller bottle. Apply to back of neck, on bones directly behind the ears, or in palms and inhale.

Target Focus

Perfect thing to keep you focused on your tasks

5 drops Orange
5 drops Peppermint

Blend Essential Oils and Fill the rest with your favorite Carrier Oil in a roller bottle. Apply to back of neck, on bones directly behind the ears, or in palms and inhale.

ATTENTION Please
Perfect to help you focus

4 drops Vetiver
3 drops Lavender
3 drops Cedarwood
3 drops Frankincense

Blend Essential Oils and Fill the rest with your favorite Carrier Oil in a roller bottle. Apply to back of neck, on bones directly behind the ears, or in palms and inhale.

Brain Power
This blend will help you sharpen your mind for more critical thinking activities.

5 drops Cedarwood
5 drops Lavender
5 drops Vetiver

Blend Essential Oils and Fill the rest with your favorite Carrier Oil in a roller bottle. Apply it through a circular motion to the temples, wrists and back of neck.

Think Tank
This blend will help you sharpen your mind for more critical thinking activities.

4 drops Rosemary
4 drops Lemon
4 drops Cypress

Blend Essential Oils and Fill the rest with your favorite Carrier Oil in a roller bottle. Apply it through a circular motion to the temples, wrists and back of neck.

Hocus Focus Magic
This helps you focus in school or work while doing your tasks

5 drops Wild Orange
5 drops Peppermint

Blend Essential Oils and Fill the rest with your favorite Carrier Oil in a roller bottle. Apply to back of neck, on bones directly behind the ears, or in palms and inhale.

Focus People Focus!

This will help you get a mental lift because this essential oil blend is great for thinking and studying.

6 drops Wild Orange
6 drops Peppermint

Blend Essential Oils and Fill the rest with your favorite Carrier Oil in a roller bottle. Apply to back of neck, on bones directly behind the ears, or in palms and inhale.

General Wellness

Toddler Ouchies Helper
Erase those bruises fast with this blend

5 drops Lavender
5 drops Melaleuca

Blend Essential Oils and Fill the rest with your favorite Carrier Oil in a roller bottle. Apply on areas that are affected.

New Skin New Life
For skin replenishing.

3 drops Lavender
3 drops Frankincense
3 drops Melaleuca
2 drops Helichrysum

Blend Essential Oils and Fill the rest with your favorite Carrier Oil in a roller bottle. Apply on areas that are affected.

Morning Alive
Get energized in the morning to have a lovely day at work.

6 drops Lemon
2 drops Eucalyptus
1 drops Peppermint
2 drops Cinnamon

Blend Essential Oils and Fill the rest with your favorite Carrier Oil in a roller bottle. Apply on your wrist, neck or feet when needed.

Itchy Witchy Away
Get the itch away with this essential oils blend

5 drops Lavender
5 drops Purification
3 drops Peppermint

Top off a 5 mL roller bottle with sweet almond oil or fractionated coconut oil. Shake and roll on!

Another great variation is substituting 3 drops of Melrose for the Peppermint.

Kiddie Owie Bomb
Heal the small bites, injuries and skin itches with this essential oil blend.

4 drops Lavender
4 drops Melaleuca

Blend Essential Oils and Fill the rest with your favorite Carrier Oil in a roller bottle. Apply on areas that are affected.

Kiddie Owie Bomb Too

Heal the small bites, injuries and skin itches with this essential oil blend.

8 drops Lavender
8 drops Melaleuca

Blend Essential Oils and Fill the rest with your favorite Carrier Oil in a roller bottle. Apply on areas that are affected.

Natural Ear Drops

Help deflate the swelling with this essential oils blend.

4 drops Purification
4 drops Lavender
4 drops Melrose
1 drops Panaway
3 drops Thyme

Blend Essential Oils and Fill the rest with your favorite Carrier Oil in a roller bottle. Apply on areas that are affected.

Bug Itchies Relief
Helps you soothe the itching from bug bites

4 drops Lavender
3 drops Chamomile
3 drops Melaleuca (Tea Tree)

Blend Essential Oils and Fill the rest with your favorite Carrier Oil in a roller bottle. Apply on areas that are affected.

Solid Nails
Perfect for giving nail support.

4 drops Lemon
3 drops Frankincense
3 drops Lavender

Blend Essential Oils and Fill the rest with your favorite Carrier Oil in a roller bottle. Apply on areas that are affected.

Protect and Live
Perfect for maintaining a good & healthy body

3 drops Lemon
3 drops Clove
3 drops Eucalyptus
3 drops Rosemary

Blend Essential Oils and Fill the rest with your favorite Carrier Oil in a roller bottle. Apply on areas that are affected.

Body Pain Wand
Perfect for taking away the pain from your body.

5 drops Lavender
5 drops Melaleuca A (tea tree)
5 drops Frankincense

Blend Essential Oils and Fill the rest with your favorite Carrier Oil in a roller bottle. Apply on areas that are affected.

Shave Saver
Perfect for your after shave regimen

2 drops Lavender
2 drops Frankincense
2 drops Myrrh
2 drops Melaleuca
2 drops Helichrysum

Blend Essential Oils and Fill the rest with your favorite Carrier Oil in a roller bottle. Apply on areas that are affected.

Bruise Almighty
Perfect remedy for bruises and cuts.

5 drops Lavender
5 drops Melaleuca or Tea Tree
5 drops Frankincense

Blend Essential Oils and Fill the rest with your favorite Carrier Oil in a roller bottle. Apply on areas that are affected.

Full Body Relaxation
Relax your mind and body with this essential oils blend.

4 drops Grapefruit
2 drops Peppermint
2 drops Rosemary
2 drops Thyme

Blend Essential Oils and Fill the rest with your favorite Carrier Oil in a roller bottle. Apply on areas that are affected.

Itchy Toddlers BFF
Stop the itching with this essential oils blend

5 drops Lavender
5 drops Purification
3 drops Peppermint

Blend Essential Oils and Fill the rest with your favorite Carrier Oil in a roller bottle. Apply on areas that are affected.

Kiddie Ouchie Helper

This essential oils blend helps lessen the discomfort felt by your children.

2 drop Lavender
2 drop Frankincense

Blend Essential Oils and Fill the rest with your favorite Carrier Oil in a roller bottle. Apply on areas that are affected.

Joy Immense

This essential oils blend will help uplift your spirit on getting well.

3 drops Lemon
2 drops Frankincense
2 drops Oregano
2 drops Thieves
2 drops Peppermint
2 drops Tea Tree

Blend Essential Oils and Fill the rest with your favorite Carrier Oil in a roller bottle. Apply it on the wrists.

No Bug Bites Today

This help bugs and insects from invading your personal space

2 drops Lemongrass,
3 drops Lavender,
2 drops Peppermint,
2 drops Cedarwood
3 drops Lavender,
3 drops Peppermint
3 drops Lemongrass

Blend Essential Oils and Fill the rest with your favorite Carrier Oil in a roller bottle. Apply on areas that are affected.

Itch Itch No Mo

This helps calm, soothe and reduce skin irritation.

4 drops Lavender
2 drops Frankincense
2 drops Peppermint
1 drop Tea Tree
1 drop Lemon

Blend Essential Oils and Fill the rest with your favorite Carrier Oil in a roller bottle. Apply on areas that are affected.

Bug Off and Away
This helps keep away insects and other bugs.

8 drops Lemon eucalyptus
4 drops Geranium
3 drops Lavender

Blend Essential Oils and Fill the rest with your favorite Carrier Oil in a roller bottle. Apply on areas that are affected.

Kiddie Bug Bite Buster
This helps soothe the itching and discomfort felt by your child from an insect bite.

2 drop Lavender
2 drop Roman Chamomile

Roll on and around bug bite area.

Iron Toe
This helps strengthen your toenails to prevent it from being brittle.

5 drops Melaleuca (Tea tree)
3 drops Lemon
2 drops Peppermint

Blend Essential Oils and Fill the rest with your favorite Carrier Oil in a roller bottle. Apply on areas that are affected.

Sexy Lippies

This helps you have your soft and healthy lips back.

3 drops Lavender
2 drops Lemon

Blend Essential Oils and Fill the rest with your favorite Carrier Oil in a roller bottle. Apply on areas that are affected.

Itch Stopper

This relieves you from the itchy feeling.

6 drops Lavender
4 drops Peppermint

Blend Essential Oils and Fill the rest with your favorite Carrier Oil in a roller bottle. Apply on areas that are affected.

Oh My Feet

This will help deflate your swollen feet and increase blood circulation, and deodorize feet.

5 drops Cypress
5 drops Peppermint

Blend Essential Oils and Fill the rest with your favorite Carrier Oil in a roller bottle. Apply on areas that are affected.

Itch Away Now

This will help stop the constant skin itching.

3 drops Lavender
3 drops Peppermint
2 drops Frankincense
2 drops Melaleuca
2 drops Lemon

Blend Essential Oils and Fill the rest with your favorite Carrier Oil in a roller bottle. Apply on areas that are affected.

Swollen Ear Care

This will help stop the ear swelling,

5 drops Melrose
5 drops Purification
5 drops Lavender
2 drops Thyme
1 drops Panaway

Blend Essential Oils and Fill the rest with your favorite Carrier Oil in a roller bottle. Apply on areas that are affected.

Body Cooler

This will help you cool down your body from a hot day outside,

7 drops Peppermint
3 drops Lavender

Blend Essential Oils and Fill the rest with your favorite Carrier Oil in a roller bottle. Apply on areas that are affected.

EO Deodorant
This will help you prevent unhealthy body odor.

4 drops Cypress
3 drops Lemongrass
3 drops Lavender

Blend Essential Oils and Fill the rest with your favorite Carrier Oil in a roller bottle. Apply on areas that are affected.

Scratch Out
This will help you stop scratching the insect and bug bites.

7 drops Purification
3 drops Lavender
3 drops Frankincense

Blend Essential Oils and Fill the rest with your favorite Carrier Oil in a roller bottle. Apply on areas that are affected.

School Study Alert

This will help your kids gain motivation and do well in school.

5 drops Peppermint
5 drops Wild Orange

Blend Essential Oils and Fill the rest with your favorite Carrier Oil in a roller bottle. Apply on your wrist or feet when needed.

Ouchie Bandit

This will help your skin recover from minor cuts, burns and bruises.

3 drops Lavender
3 drops Frankincense
3 drops Tea Tree
2 drops Helichrysum

Blend Essential Oils and Fill the rest with your favorite Carrier Oil in a roller bottle. Apply on areas that are affected.

Happy

Mood Uplift

This will help you lift up your mood and fill your day with positivity.

5 drops Trauma Life
2 drops Sara
2 drops Release
2 drops Hope
2 drops Joy
2 drops Frankincense
2 drops Lavender

Blend Essential Oils and Fill the rest with your favorite Carrier Oil in a roller bottle. Apply it on the wrists.

The Energizer Puppy

Get energized with this essential oils blend/

5 drops Lime
4 drops Lemon
1 drops Peppermint

Add the Drops of each Young Living Essential Oil and fill the reminder with carrier oil. Do Not overfill you need space to put the top on!

Power Up Pill

Get energized with this essential oils blend/

6 drops Rosemary
4 drops Peppermint
4 drops Grapefruit

Add the Drops of each Young Living Essential Oil and fill the reminder with carrier oil. Do Not overfill you need space to put the top on!

Kid's Happy Pill

Help bring back your kiddo's positive attitude with this essential oils blend.

4 drops White Angelica
4 drops Stress Away

Blend Essential Oils and Fill the rest with your favorite Carrier Oil in a roller bottle. Apply it on the wrists.

Teacher Power Puff

Helps teachers stay energized for various activities and events in and out of the school.

1 1/2 teaspoons fractionated coconut oil
8 drops Orange
4 drops Cardamom
3 drops Thieves

Blend Essential Oils and Fill the rest with your favorite Carrier Oil in a roller bottle. Apply it on the wrists.

Happy Happy Joy Joy
This blend is perfect for uplifting one's mood and spirit.

4 drops CitrusBliss
4 drops Elevation
5 drops Frankincense
2 drops Peppermint
2 drops Patchouli

Joy to Me
This essential oils blend will help you uplift your mood

3 drops Grapefruit
3 drops Wild Orange
2 drops Lemon
1 drops Bergamot

Blend Essential Oils and Fill the rest with your favorite Carrier Oil in a roller bottle. Apply to back of neck, on bones directly behind the ears, or in palms and inhale.

Madness Begone
This helps the mind ease away the anger.

7 drops Serenity
7 drops Balance

Blend Essential Oils and Fill the rest with your favorite Carrier Oil in a roller bottle. Apply it on the wrists.

Bottled Happy
This is your happy pill in a bottle,

2 drops Joy
4 drops Peppermint
5 drops Lemon
5 drops Tangerine

Blend Essential Oils and Fill the rest with your favorite Carrier Oil in a roller bottle. Apply it on the wrists.

Headaches

Flexi Neck

Ease the neck and head tension with this DIY essential oils blend.

2 drops Copaiba
2 drops Peppermint
2 drops Wintergreen
2 drops Marjoram
3 drops Lavender
3 drops Eucalyptus Globolus

Blend Essential Oils and Fill the rest with your favorite Carrier Oil in a roller bottle. Apply it through a circular motion to the temples and back of neck.

Fast Drip Pain Relief

Perfect for immediate relief on headaches and tensions.

6 drops M-Grain
4 drops PanAway
4 drops Peppermint
4 drops Valor

Blend Essential Oils and Fill the rest with your favorite Carrier Oil in a roller bottle. Apply it through a circular motion to the temples and back of neck.

Tense Head Tamer
Relieve Tension Headaches in a Jiffy

3 drops Peppermint
2 drops Clove
3 drops Wintergreen
2 drops Ginger

Blend Essential Oils and Fill the rest with your favorite Carrier Oil in a roller bottle. Apply it through a circular motion to the temples and back of neck.

Relaxing Head Banging
Stop the never-ending head pounding and relax yourself with this essential oils blend

4 drops Lavender
4 drops Frankincense
4 drops Copaiba
4 drops Peppermint

Blend Essential Oils and Fill the rest with your favorite Carrier Oil in a roller bottle. Apply it through a circular motion to the temples and back of neck.

Enough Pounding Headaches

Stop your head from pounding with this essential oils blend

5 drops Peppermint
5 drops Frankincense
5 drops Lavender

Blend Essential Oils and Fill the rest with your favorite Carrier Oil in a roller bottle. Apply it through a circular motion to the temples and back of neck.

Head Neck Soothe

This helps relieves head and neck tension.

4 drops Peppermint
2 drops Frankincense
2 drops Lavender
2 drops Chamomile

Blend Essential Oils and Fill the rest with your favorite Carrier Oil in a roller bottle. Apply it through a circular motion to the temples and back of neck.

Migraine Magic Wand

This is a great help for people who experience headaches and migraines.

5 drops PanAway
5 drops Valor
4 drops Copaiba
4 drops Peppermint

Blend Essential Oils and Fill the rest with your favorite Carrier Oil in a roller bottle. Apply it through a circular motion to the temples and back of neck.

Deep Meditation Potion

This is perfect for yoga practices because it can help deepen meditation and enhance the feeling of groundedness.

3 drops Frankincense
2 drops Lavender
2 drops Sacred Mountain
2 drops Valor
2 drops Royal Hawaiian Sandalwood

Blend Essential Oils and Fill the rest with your favorite Carrier Oil in a roller bottle. Apply it through a circular motion to the temples and back of neck.

Pounding Headache Go
This will help ease the constant headaches you experience

4 drops Peppermint
3 drops Basil
3 drops Lemongrass
4 drops Frankincense

Blend Essential Oils and Fill the rest with your favorite Carrier Oil in a roller bottle. Apply it through a circular motion to the temples and back of neck.

Vertigo Schmertigo
This will help you increase blood flow and improve your airways and lessen dizziness and nausea.

2 drops Frankincense
2 drops Lavender
4 drops Cypress
1 drop Ginger
1 drop Peppermint

Blend Essential Oils and Fill the rest with your favorite Carrier Oil in a roller bottle. Apply it through a circular motion to the temples and back of neck.

No Tension Today

This will help you relax, calm, and ease head and neck tension.

5 drops Lavender
3 drops Peppermint
2 drops Eucalyptus

Blend Essential Oils and Fill the rest with your favorite Carrier Oil in a roller bottle. Apply it through a circular motion to the temples and back of neck.

Headache Hammer

This will save the fam from any constant head banging feeling experiences

4 drops Frankincense
4 drops Lavender
4 drops Peppermint

Blend Essential Oils and Fill the rest with your favorite Carrier Oil in a roller bottle. Apply it through a circular motion to the temples and back of neck.

Immune System

Immuno Hero

Boost your immune system for a productive day at work or in school.

3 drops Oregano
5 drops Lemon
4 drops On Guard
4 drops Melaleuca (tea tree oil)

Blend Essential Oils and Fill the rest with your favorite Carrier Oil in a roller bottle. Apply onto chest and/or back. Can also apply to the tops of feet at the bridge of the toes.

Super Immunity Power

Boost your immune system with this essential oil blend.

4 drops Frankincense
4 drops Lemon
4 drops Melaleuca Tea Tree
4 drops Protective Blend
Fractionated Coconut oil

Applying this every few hours along my spine will help boost your immune support.

Immunity Booster Power

Helps boost your immune system for a productive day.

3 drops Oregano
3 drops Melaleuca
3 drops Lemon
3 drops Frankincense
3 drops Cinnamon

Blend Essential Oils and Fill the rest with your favorite Carrier Oil in a roller bottle. Apply onto chest and/or back. Can also apply to the tops of feet at the bridge of the toes.

Immunity Special Powers

Support and boost your immune system with this essential oils blend.

4 drops Orange
4 drops Lemon
4 drops Thieves
4 drops Frankincense

Blend Essential Oils and Fill the rest with your favorite Carrier Oil in a roller bottle. Apply onto chest and/or back. Can also apply to the tops of feet at the bridge of the toes.

Immune System Upgrade
Support and boost your immune system
with this essential oils blend.

5 drops Thieves
5 drops Purification
5 drops Oregano

Blend Essential Oils and Fill the rest with
your favorite Carrier Oil in a roller bottle.
Apply onto chest and/or back. Can also apply
to the tops of feet at the bridge of the toes.

Respiratory Protect
This creates a soothing aroma that can help
your respiratory system function well.

8 drops Respiratory Blend
5 drops Eucalyptus
4 drops Frankincense

Blend Essential Oils and Fill the rest with
your favorite Carrier Oil in a roller bottle.
Apply onto chest and/or back. Can also apply
to the tops of feet at the bridge of the toes.

Kiddie Respiratory Boost

This essential oils blend helps support your child's respiratory health.

2 drop Cardamom
2 drop Frankincense

Blend Essential Oils and Fill the rest with your favorite Carrier Oil in a roller bottle. Apply onto chest and/or back. Can also apply to the tops of feet at the bridge of the toes.

Captain Immunity Power

This helps support healthy immune functions.

2 drops Oregano
2 drops Tea Tree
2 drops Lemon
2 drops Frankincense
2 drops Cinnamon

Blend Essential Oils and Fill the rest with your favorite Carrier Oil in a roller bottle. Apply onto chest and/or back. Can also apply to the tops of feet at the bridge of the toes.

Breathe Easy & Right
This will help you breathe without having difficulties

4 drops Peppermint
2 drops Eucalyptus
2 drops Lemon
2 drops Rosemary

Blend Essential Oils and Fill the rest with your favorite Carrier Oil in a roller bottle. Apply onto chest and/or back. Can also apply to the tops of feet at the bridge of the toes.

Respiratory Helper
This will help you fight the motion sickness when traveling to far places.

5 drops Lemon
6 drops Lavender
5 drops Peppermint

Blend Essential Oils and Fill the rest with your favorite Carrier Oil in a roller bottle. Apply onto palms of hands, cup, and inhale.

Health Protect and Prevent

This will help you prevent from having chronic illnesses.

7 drops Peace & Calming
5 drops Lavender
5 drops Frankincense

Blend Essential Oils and Fill the rest with your favorite Carrier Oil in a roller bottle. Apply onto chest and/or back. Can also apply to the tops of feet at the bridge of the toes.

Motion Sickness

Jet Lag? What's That?
Get energized after a long travel period with this essential oils blend.

2 drops Sweet or Wild Orange
2 drops Frankincense
2 drops Peppermint
2 drops Eucalyptus
2 drops Rosemary

to use: apply over heart and to pulse points behind ears and on wrists. rub wrists together and deeply inhale aroma, making an effort to breathe deeply and intentionally for several seconds.

Let's get Motivated
Get that motivation to do well on your tasks with this essential oils blend.

4 drops Black Pepper
4 drops Lime
4 drops Orange
4 drops Frankincense

Top off a 5 or 10 mL bottle with almond oil, grape seed or fractionated coconut oil. Roll on wrists 2 times a day!

Blah Feeling Away
Helps you take away the feeling of nausea.

5 drops Lavender
5 drops Lemon
5 drops Peppermint

Blend Essential Oils and Fill the rest with your favorite Carrier Oil in a roller bottle. Apply onto chest and/or back. Can also apply to the tops of feet at the bridge of the toes.

No More Motion Icky
This helps prevent any motion sickness when traveling to far places by car, plane or ship.

5 drops Peppermint
3 drops Lavender
2 drops Ginger

To use: apply to inner wrists, rub them together, and then bring wrists close to nose and breathe in deeply for several counts followed by exhaling for several counts.

Smooth Motion
This will help everyone not miss the fun and adventures while traveling.

8 drops Peppermint
8 drops Ginger

Blend Essential Oils and Fill the rest with your favorite Carrier Oil in a roller bottle. Apply on the back of the neck, wrists and apply it clockwise on the tummy area.

Seasick Protection
This will help the motion sickness while traveling by boat.

5 drops Thieves
3 drops Purification
3 drops Frankincense
2 drops Lemon
2 drops Oregano

Blend Essential Oils and Fill the rest with your favorite Carrier Oil in a roller bottle. Apply onto chest and/or back. Can also apply to the tops of feet at the bridge of the toes.

Muscle Care

Athletic Muscle Helper

After a long, tiring game, this will help your body heal and eases the muscle tension you feel.,

5 drops Frankincense
4 drops Lemongrass
2 drops Marjoram
5 drops Peppermint.

Blend Essential Oils and Fill the rest with your favorite Carrier Oil in a roller bottle. Apply on areas that are affected with muscle contraction.

Body Ache Combat

After pounding yourself at work, we guarantee you that this essential oil blend will be your newest best friend.

5 drops Eucalyptus
5 drops Lavender
5 drops Deep Blue

Blend Essential Oils and Fill the rest with your favorite Carrier Oil in a roller bottle. Apply on areas that are affected with muscle contraction.

Muscle Heal

Ease the muscle pain away to be more productive the next day.

3 drops Clove
3 drops Black Pepper
5 drops Peppermint
5 drops Wintergreen

Blend Essential Oils and Fill the rest with your favorite Carrier Oil in a roller bottle. Apply on areas that are affected with muscle contraction.

Achy Breaky Muscles

Ease the tough muscle pain and get more energy the next day at work or in school.

8 drops Peppermint
8 drops Lavender

Blend Essential Oils and Fill the rest with your favorite Carrier Oil in a roller bottle. Apply on areas that are affected with muscle contraction.

Upper Body Power
Helps lessen the back, shoulders, and neck pains

5 drops Peppermint
2 drops Clove
5 drops Wintergreen
2 drops Black Pepper
5 drops Lemongrass

Blend Essential Oils and Fill the rest with your favorite Carrier Oil in a roller bottle. Apply on areas that are affected with muscle contraction.

Muscle Ache Combat
Soothe the aching muscles with this essential oils blend

3 drops Valor or Valor ll
3 drops wintergreen
3 drops Panaway
3 drops Copaiba
3 drops of Relieve it

Blend Essential Oils and Fill the rest with your favorite Carrier Oil in a roller bottle. Apply on areas that are affected with muscle contraction.

Muscle Soother Pal

Soothe the muscle pain away with this essential oil blend.

3 drops Wintergreen
3 drops Peppermint
2 drops Juniper
2 drops Lemongrass

Blend Essential Oils and Fill the rest with your favorite Carrier Oil in a roller bottle. Apply on areas that are affected with muscle contraction.

Muscle Tension Tamer

This helps in soothing tensioned muscles.

5 drops Wintergreen
5 drops Valor
5 drops Peppermint
5 drops Panaway

Blend Essential Oils and Fill the rest with your favorite Carrier Oil in a roller bottle. Apply on areas that are affected with muscle contraction.

Soothe Thy Muscle
This helps soothe the muscle contractions.

4 drops Peppermint
4 drops Panaway
4 drops Valor
4 drops Wintergreen

Blend Essential Oils and Fill the rest with your favorite Carrier Oil in a roller bottle. Apply on areas that are affected with muscle contraction.

Tight Muscle Release
This will help you soothe muscle tensions.

6 drops Peppermint
2 drops Black Pepper
2 drops Clove

Blend Essential Oils and Fill the rest with your favorite Carrier Oil in a roller bottle. Apply on areas that are affected with muscle contraction.

Adventurer's Muscle Buddy
This will help you soothe the aching muscles after a day of adventure

3 drops Wintergreen
3 drops Peppermint
2 drops Juniper Berry
2 drops Lemongrass

Blend Essential Oils and Fill the rest with your favorite Carrier Oil in a roller bottle. Apply on areas that are affected with muscle contraction.

Pain Buster
This will help you ease the constant pain you are feeling.

4 drops Marjoram
4 drops Lemongrass
4 drops Frankincense

Blend Essential Oils and Fill the rest with your favorite Carrier Oil in a roller bottle. Apply on areas that are affected.

Skin Care

Hot Summer Heat Cooler
Feel cooled and refreshed on a hot summer day with this essential oils blend.

3 drops Peppermint
3 drops Spearmint
2 drops Eucalyptus
2 drops Lavender

Blend Essential Oils and Fill the rest with your favorite Carrier Oil in a roller bottle. Apply on areas that are affected.

Black and Purple Eraser
Have that bruise gone in no time with this essential oils blend.

5 drops Panaway
3 drops Lavender
3 drops Copaiba
4 drops Cypress

Blend Essential Oils and Fill the rest with your favorite Carrier Oil in a roller bottle. Apply on areas that are affected.

Black and Purple Eraser 2.0
Have that bruise gone in no time with this essential oils blend.

5 drops Lavender
5 drops Geranium
2 drops Helichrysum
2 drops Frankincense

Blend Essential Oils and Fill the rest with your favorite Carrier Oil in a roller bottle. Apply on areas that are affected.

Crystal Skin
Have that healthy and clear skin with this essential oils blend.

4 drops Melaleuca (Tea Tree)
4 drops Lemon
2 drops Lavender

Blend Essential Oils and Fill the rest with your favorite Carrier Oil in a roller bottle. Apply on areas that are affected.

Skin Fixer Up
Have that healthy and flawless skin back with this essential oil blend .

5 drops Geranium
4 drops Frankincense
6 drops Lavender

Blend Essential Oils and Fill the rest with your favorite Carrier Oil in a roller bottle. Apply on areas that are affected.

Banish Black and Blue
Have that healthy glowing skin back with no worries with this essential oil blend.

6 drops Lavender
6 drops Cypress
6 drops Frankincense

Blend Essential Oils and Fill the rest with your favorite Carrier Oil in a roller bottle. Apply on areas that are affected.

Skin Repair
Perfect for skin healing

4 drops Frankincense
2 drops Melaleuca
3 drops Lavender

Blend Essential Oils and Fill the rest with your favorite Carrier Oil in a roller bottle. Apply on areas that are affected.

Scar Eraser
This helps get rid of scars.

3 drops Frankincense
5 drops Helichrysum
3 drops Myrrh
3 drops Lavender

Blend Essential Oils and Fill the rest with your favorite Carrier Oil in a roller bottle. Apply on areas that are affected.

Sun Shield
This is perfect as a sunblock substitute, it helps soothe the skin after a day in the sun.

5 drops Lavender
3 drops Helichrysum
3 drops Peppermint

Blend Essential Oils and Fill the rest with your favorite Carrier Oil in a roller bottle. Apply on areas that are affected.

Bruise Busters

This will help on healing bruised skin.

4 drops Lavender
4 drops Helichrysum
2 drops Fennel

Blend Essential Oils and Fill the rest with your favorite Carrier Oil in a roller bottle. Apply on areas that are affected.

Sunburn Burn Away

This will help them sunburn heal faster.

5 drops Frankincense
3 drops Myrrh
3 drops Geranium
3 drops Lavender

Blend Essential Oils and Fill the rest with your favorite Carrier Oil in a roller bottle. Apply on areas that are affected.

Face Toner Express

This will help you even your complexion in no time.

5 drops Purification
5 drops Lemon
5 drops Tea Tree

Blend Essential Oils and Fill the rest with your favorite Carrier Oil in a roller bottle. Apply on areas that are affected.

Facial Magic

This will help you even your complexion in no time.

5 drops Lavender
5 drops Frankincense
5 drops Tea Tree

Blend Essential Oils and Fill the rest with your favorite Carrier Oil in a roller bottle. Apply on areas that are affected.

So Fresh and So Calm

This will help you feel refreshed and calmed.

6 drops Lavender
4 drops Spearmint

Blend Essential Oils and Fill the rest with your favorite Carrier Oil in a roller bottle. Apply on areas that are affected.

Heal Skin

This will help your skin heal from bug bites and irritated skin.

5 drops Lavender
5 drops Purification
3 drops Tea Tree

Blend Essential Oils and Fill the rest with your favorite Carrier Oil in a roller bottle. Apply on areas that are affected.

Sleep

Good Night Lights Out
Doze off soundly with this essential oil blend,

4 drops Roman Chamomile
5 drops Bergamot
6 drops Frankincense

Blend Essential Oils and Fill the rest with your favorite Carrier Oil in a roller bottle. Apply on your hands and rub them together, while breathing in the aroma.

Goodbye Sneezes
Get away from sleepless nights with this blend. This will help you calm your body to have that good night sleep.

1 drops Marjoram
3 drops Frankincense
3 drops Bergamot
4 drops Roman Chamomile
4 drops Vetiver
6 drops Lavender
3 drops Cedarwood

Blend Essential Oils and Fill the rest with your favorite Carrier Oil in a roller bottle. Apply on your hands and rub them together, while breathing in the aroma.

Sweet Sleepy Nights

Get that sweet and restful sleep with this essential oils blend.

5 drops Lavender
5 drops Cedarwood
2 drops Bergamot

Blend Essential Oils and Fill the rest with your favorite Carrier Oil in a roller bottle. Apply on your hands and rub them together, while breathing in the aroma.

Stop the SNORE

Have a good night sleep without the snoring with this essential oils blend

4 drops Marjoram
4 drops Geranium
2 drops Cedarwood
1 drops Frankincense
1 drops Eucalyptus Radiata
4 drops Lavender

Blend Essential Oils and Fill the rest with your favorite Carrier Oil in a roller bottle. Apply on your hands and rub them together, while breathing in the aroma.

Sleep Like a Log
Have good night of sleep with this essential oils blend.

5 drops Lavender
5 drops Cedarwood

Blend Essential Oils and Fill the rest with your favorite Carrier Oil in a roller bottle. Apply on your hands and rub them together, while breathing in the aroma.

40 Winks Guaranteed
Nap soundly with this essential oils blend.

10 drops Lavender
7 drops Vetiver
2 drops Roman Chamomile

Blend Essential Oils and Fill the rest with your favorite Carrier Oil in a roller bottle. Apply on your hands and rub them together, while breathing in the aroma.

Happy Zzzzzs
Perfect for a good night sleep

5 drops Lavender
5 drops Bergamot
10 drops Cedarwood

Blend Essential Oils and Fill the rest with your favorite Carrier Oil in a roller bottle. Apply on your hands and rub them together, while breathing in the aroma.

Relax Sleep
This helps your body relax and sleep easily.

4 drops Lavender
3 drops Geranium
3 drops Roman Chamomile

Blend Essential Oils and Fill the rest with your favorite Carrier Oil in a roller bottle. Apply on your hands and rub them together, while breathing in the aroma.

Kiddie Sleepy Time
This helps your child relax and sleep well.

3 drop Lavender
2 drop Cedarwood

Blend Essential Oils and Fill the rest with your favorite Carrier Oil in a roller bottle. Apply on your hands and rub them together, while breathing in the aroma.

Sweet Dreams Nightly
This will help you have the sweetest of dream you will ever have.

4 drops Lavender
4 drops Cedarwood
4 drops Valor
4 drops Orange

Blend Essential Oils and Fill the rest with your favorite Carrier Oil in a roller bottle. Apply on your hands and rub them together, while breathing in the aroma.

Travel Must Have

This will help you recover from jet lag and from a stressful day of travel

4 drops Lavender
3 drops Cedarwood
3 drops Vetiver

Blend Essential Oils and Fill the rest with your favorite Carrier Oil in a roller bottle. Apply on your hands and rub them together, while breathing in the aroma.

Snooze Away

When your kiddo can't sleep because he is afraid of the jeepers creepers, this blend is perfect for you.

6 drops Lavender
4 drops Serenity
2 drops Roman Chamomile

Blend Essential Oils and Fill the rest with your favorite Carrier Oil in a roller bottle. Apply on your hands and rub them together, while breathing in the aroma.

Stomach Care

Very Belly Good
Ease the tummy ache away and enjoy the rest of the day.

5ml Sample Recipe
8 drops Wild Orange
8 drops Digestive Blend

Blend Essential Oils and Fill the rest with your favorite Carrier Oil in a roller bottle. Apply on the back of the neck, wrists and apply it clockwise on the tummy area.

Toddler Tummy Tamer
Help take away of your child's tummy aches with this essential oils blend.

5 drops Lemon
5 drops Copaiba

Add to 5 mL bottle and top off with carrier oil.

My Tummy Feels Great
Perfect tummy ache reliever

3 drops Ginger
2 drops Peppermint
2 drops Fennel
1 drops Coriander
1 drops Lemon

Blend Essential Oils and Fill the rest with your favorite Carrier Oil in a roller bottle. Apply on the back of the neck, wrists and apply it clockwise on the tummy area.

Feel Good Tummy
Stop the tummy ache with this essential oils blend.

4 drops Lavender
3 drops Peppermint
3 drops Ginger

Roll on belly and massage in a clockwise circular motion.

Kiddie Tummy Happy
This helps give your child a healthy digestion.

2 drop Cardamom
2 drop Orange

Blend Essential Oils and Fill the rest with your favorite Carrier Oil in a roller bottle. Apply on the back of the neck, wrists and apply it clockwise on the tummy area.

PMS Pal
This helps put away the abdomen cramps.

5 drops PanAway
5 drops Lemongrass
5 drops Copaiba

Blend Essential Oils and Fill the rest with your favorite Carrier Oil in a roller bottle. Apply on the back of the neck, wrists and apply it clockwise on the tummy area.

My Tummy Paradise
This will help ease nausea and upset stomachs.

4 drops Ginger
3 drops Fennel
3 drops Peppermint

Blend Essential Oils and Fill the rest with your favorite Carrier Oil in a roller bottle. Apply on the back of the neck, wrists and apply it clockwise on the tummy area.

Tummy Pain Away
This will help ease the pain of the endless tummy aches

7 drops Peppermint
7 drops Ginger

Blend Essential Oils and Fill the rest with your favorite Carrier Oil in a roller bottle. Apply on the back of the neck, wrists and apply it clockwise on the tummy area.

My Tummy Goody

This will help you heal the tummy aches you are feeling.

8 drops Fennel
7 drops Wild Orange

Blend Essential Oils and Fill the rest with your favorite Carrier Oil in a roller bottle. Apply on the back of the neck, wrists and apply it clockwise on the tummy area.

Goodbye Upset Tummy

Upset tummy no more with this essential oils blend.

3 drops DiGize
3 drops Peppermint
2 drops Fennel

Top off a 5 mL bottle with sweet almond oil or fractionated coconut oil! Rub on tummy 2-3 times a day.

Stress Relief

Teacher Chill

After a long stressful day in school, you
deserve to relax and calm yourself for
another day is coming.

1 1/2 teaspoons fractionated coconut oil
6 drops Ylang Ylang
5 drops Clary Sage
4 drops Royal Hawaiian Sandalwood

Blend Essential Oils and Fill the rest with
your favorite Carrier Oil in a roller bottle.
Apply on wrists or back of neck as desired

Stress Combat

Calm your mind and senses with this
essential oil blend

5 drops Bergamot
5 drops Frankincense

Blend Essential Oils and Fill the rest with
your favorite Carrier Oil in a roller bottle.
Apply on wrists or back of neck as desired

Body Relaxation & Grounding
Relax your whole body with this essential oil blend

1 drops Patchouli
1 drops Vetiver
1 drops Lime
10 drops Balance
10 drops Lavender

Blend Essential Oils and Fill the rest with your favorite Carrier Oil in a roller bottle. Apply on wrists or back of neck as desired

My Personal Destresser
Take the stress away from your system with this essential oils blend.

5 drops Stress Away
2 drops Lavender
2 drops Frankincense
2 drops Patchouli
1 drops Valor
1 drops White Angelica

Blend Essential Oils and Fill the rest with your favorite Carrier Oil in a roller bottle. Apply on wrists or back of neck as desired

Alive Energy
This great for fighting the exhausting feeling you are experiencing

7 drops Eucalyptus Radiata
5 drops Rosemary
3 drops Grapefruit

Blend Essential Oils and Fill the rest with your favorite Carrier Oil in a roller bottle. Apply on wrists or back of neck as desired

Mommy Stress Tamer
This helps mommy calm themselves and bid the stress farewell.

6 drops Frankincense
5 drops Bergamot
3 drops Orange
3 drops Grapefruit
3 drops Clary Sage

Blend Essential Oils and Fill the rest with your favorite Carrier Oil in a roller bottle. Apply on wrists or back of neck as desired

Stress-free Zone Today

This will help get away from the stress you are experiencing today.

5 drops Eucalyptus
5 drops Spearmint

Blend Essential Oils and Fill the rest with your favorite Carrier Oil in a roller bottle. Apply on wrists or back of neck as desired

Stress Out and Away

This will help some of your mama dramas when things are starting to get tough

3 drops Balance
3 drops Serenity
3 drops Lavender
3 drops Grapefruit or Citrus Bliss
2 drops Wild Orange

Blend Essential Oils and Fill the rest with your favorite Carrier Oil in a roller bottle. Apply on wrists or back of neck as desired

Throw In the Towel and Unwind
This will help you meditate and relax your body after a long and tiring day

3 drops Orange
3 drops Lemon
3 drops Grapefruit
3 drops Bergamot
4 drops Clary Sage
4 drops Frankincense

Blend Essential Oils and Fill the rest with your favorite Carrier Oil in a roller bottle. Apply on wrists or back of neck as desired

Nerve Relief
Turn your nerve-wracking day into a calm and peaceful day with this essential oils blend.

5 drops Lavender
5 drops Valor
3 drops Vetiver
3 drops Grapefruit
3 drops Joy
2 drops Release
2 drops Cedarwood

Blend Essential Oils and Fill the rest with your favorite Carrier Oil in a roller bottle. Apply on wrists or back of neck as desired

Peace and Calm

With all your mama stress, this can help you get some peace and calm

3 drops Sandalwood
3 drops Ylang Ylang
3 drops Cypress
3 drops Bergamot
3 drops Black Pepper

Blend Essential Oils and Fill the rest with your favorite Carrier Oil in a roller bottle. Apply on wrists or back of neck as desired

My Most Favorite Roller Recipes

Use the pages following to document your own blends and the ones that work best for you

My Most Favorite Roller Recipes

My Most Favorite
Roller Recipes

My Most Favorite Roller Recipes

My Most Favorite Roller Recipes

My Most Favorite Roller Recipes

My Most Favorite Roller Recipes

My Most Favorite Roller Recipes

My Most Favorite
Roller Recipes

My Most Favorite Roller Recipes

My Most Favorite
Roller Recipes

My Most Favorite Roller Recipes

Book Ordering

To order your copy / copies of
Roller Recipes for Essential Oils

please visit:
OilNaturalEmpress.com

You can also check out other titles available.

Bulk Pricing and
Affiliate Programs Available

Made in the USA
Columbia, SC
12 March 2020